Visit a tavern that welcomed George Washington. Meander through the grand homes and gardens of men who risked their fortunes and their lives by signing the Declaration of Independence. Sit in a classroom where young Francis Scott Key may have written his first poetry. Bow your head before the crypt of John Paul Jones. Follow the paths taken by George Dewey, "Bull" Halsey, and Chester Nimitz. Most of all, consider the ideas that were nurtured in the tiny city of Annapolis: the idea that all men are equal and should govern themselves, the idea that people should be free to practice the religion of their choice, the idea that a new nation made up of descendants of immigrants who arrived on its shores mainly in steerage might become the greatest naval power in the world.

Sailors from around the world come to Annapolis to participate in yachting events. But on Wednesday nights in the summer, it's mostly locals competing in races sponsored by the venerable Annapolis Yacht Club.

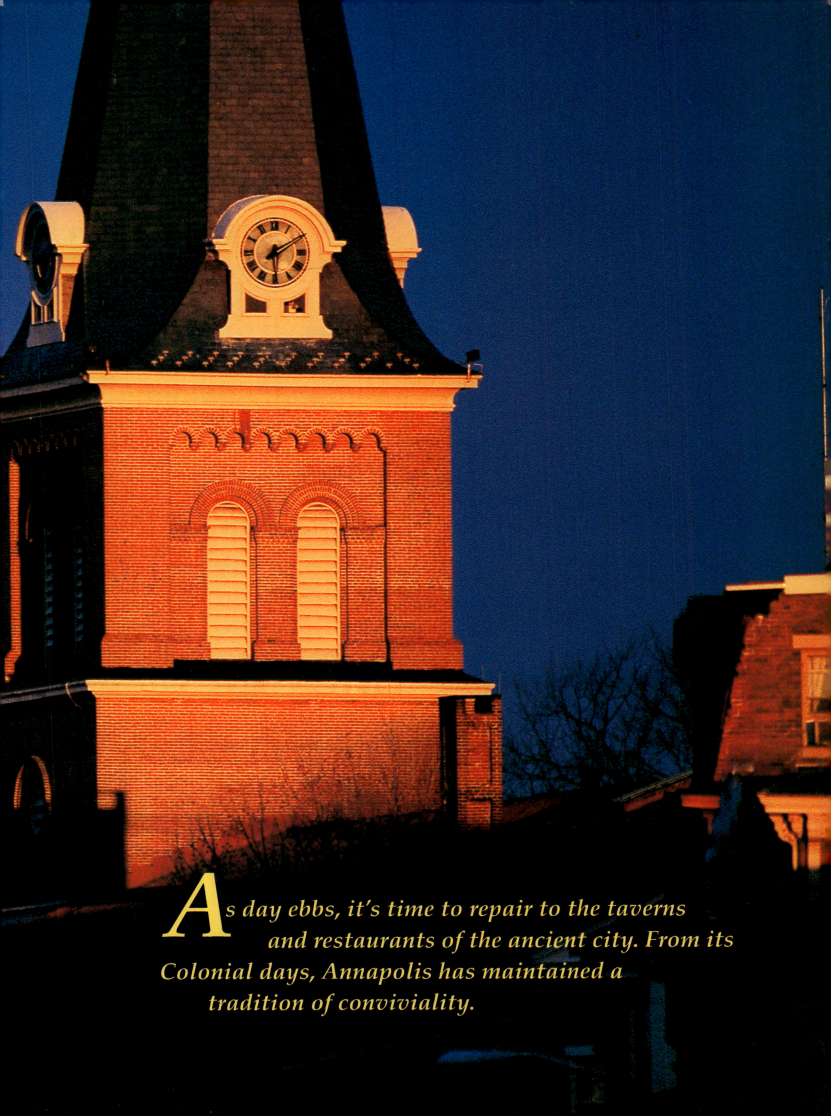

*A*s day ebbs, it's time to repair to the taverns and restaurants of the ancient city. From its Colonial days, Annapolis has maintained a tradition of conviviality.

▲ *Spa Creek divides downtown Annapolis from Eastport, once a working-class neighborhood of watermen and boatyard workers. Today, Eastport is home to more recreational yachts than working boats.*

Front cover: St. Anne's Church, the Maryland State House, and the Naval Academy Chapel form a line from the heart of town to the Severn River. Inside front cover: Only Bill XXVII, the mascot, remains impassive among thousands cheering Navy's football team. Pages 2/3: Many a sun has set on the old bricks of Annapolis where hundreds of 18th-century buildings remain intact. Pages 4/5: Spa Creek. Photos by Kevin T. Gilbert.

Annapolis, settled in 1649, is in Maryland on the eastern seaboard of the United States.

Edited by Cheri C. Madison.
Book design by K. C. DenDooven.

First Printing, 1996.
DESTINATION - ANNAPOLIS: THE STORY BEHIND THE SCENERY.
© 1996 KC PUBLICATIONS, INC.

LC96-75073. ISBN 0-88714-107-2.

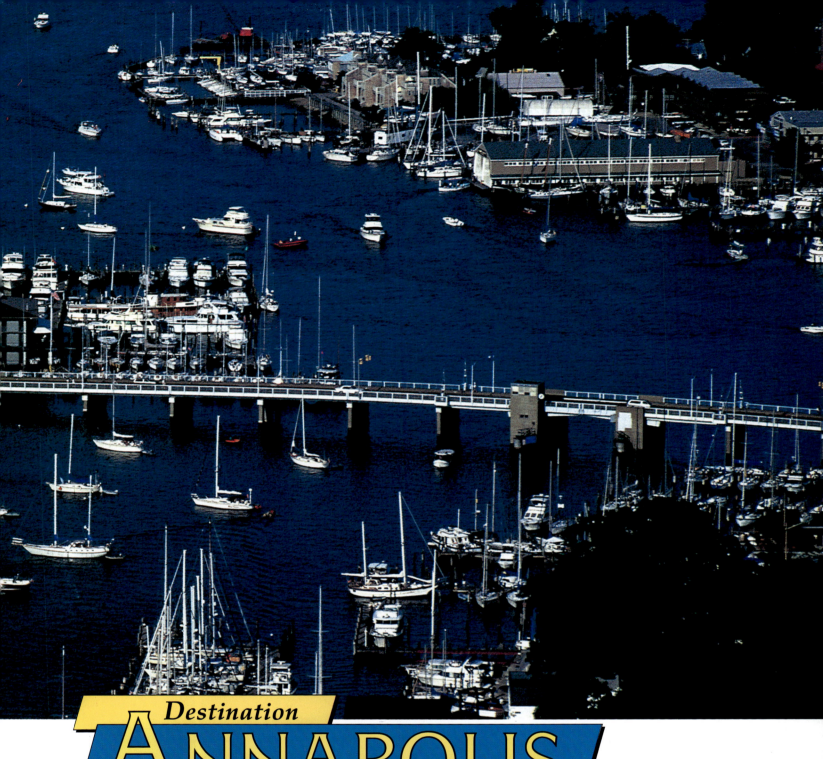

Destination ANNAPOLIS
THE STORY BEHIND THE SCENERY®

by Philip M. Evans

As a journalist, Philip M. Evans has been writing about the state of Maryland and the city of Annapolis for over four decades.

photographers: Kevin T. Gilbert & Celia Pearson

Eleven-year Annapolis resident Kevin T. Gilbert is Chief Photographer for the Washington Times Newspaper. Celia Pearson, Annapolis free-lance photographer for sixteen years, specializes in architectural and garden photography.

*"Government became the business
of the town; politics became its
vocation and avocation."*

The Founding of Annapolis

In 1608, when Captain John Smith became the first European to see the upper Chesapeake Bay, he wrote: "Heaven and earth have never agreed better to frame a place for man's habitation." In 1649, the first English settlers to arrive in the Annapolis area found an environment that lived up in every way to Smith's promise.

The few Indians the settlers encountered were peaceable. The climate was mild. The land the settlers cleared to plant crops proved fertile. The numerous creeks and bays along which they built about ten widely-dispersed homes offered safe harbor and easy access to

◀ **When Captain John** Smith explored the Chesapeake Bay, he found a land both beautiful and hospitable. Except for the spans of the Chesapeake Bay Bridge, on a misty morning the bay and the Severn River look not unlike the panorama seen by Smith in 1608.

The first settlers ▶ of Annapolis were fleeing religious persecution. More often than not, contemporary settlers are fleeing the problems of urban living. Annapolis offers them modern condominiums for waterfront living, and, as it has since Colonial times, safe harbor for their boats.

the shipping lanes to Europe and the West Indies.

These first English settlers were Puritans who were victims of religious persecution in Virginia. They fled to Maryland, a colony presided over by Cecil Calvert, 2nd Lord Baltimore. Although Calvert was a Roman Catholic, Maryland had a tradition of religious toleration. In fact, the very year that the Puritans arrived, the provincial Assembly approved Maryland's "Act Concerning Religion," allowing members of various Christian sects to practice their faith without official harassment.

The Puritans settled around Greenbury Point and Whitehall Bay on the north shore of the Severn, opposite the site of the current Annapolis. They called their settlement Providence.

Unfortunately, the declaration of religious toleration did little to assure it. The early years of the settlement at Providence were marked by repeated disputes between the Puritans and the mostly Roman Catholic authorities in the provincial capital of Maryland, St. Mary's, on the Potomac River about 55 miles to the south.

In 1654, the ongoing strife came to a head when the provincial governor, William Stone, led an expedition of 130 men from St. Mary's against the Puritans. Stone landed his party at Horn Point on the opposite bank of the Severn from Providence. On the following day, the Puritans crossed the Severn upriver and marched six miles overland to surprise Stone's force from the rear. The Puritans killed about 50 of Stone's men, captured most of the survivors, and executed 10 of them. Three years passed before Lord Baltimore regained control of his colony.

War swirled around Annapolis during the Revolution, the War of 1812, and the Civil War, but the only fighting ever to occur in the immediate environs of the city was the Battle of the Severn.

In the 1650s, land was surveyed on the south side of the Severn in what now is Annapolis. It became known as The Town at Proctor's. A new county, named Anne Arundel after the wife of the 2nd Lord Baltimore, was created embracing Providence, Proctor's, and the surrounding area.

As fast as land could be cleared, the early settlers planted tobacco. Demand for the crop in Europe seemed insatiable. Tobacco had to be shipped to England, and the settlers needed English goods. Proctor's offered a more protected port than Providence.

By the latter half of the 17th century, the Maryland Assembly had begun to question the viability of St. Mary's as the capital. Assembly

▲ **Harvesting the riches of Chesapeake Bay** and its tributaries is done for commercial profit and family fun. In Colonial times, the bay offered a constant source of food in years when crops failed. Recently, pollution and shellfish disease have depleted harvests of fin fish, crabs, and oysters. The Chesapeake Bay Foundation, based in Annapolis, is waging a campaign to clean up the bay, with some positive results.

▲ **Like spokes of a wheel, the streets of Annapolis radiate from State Circle just as Governor Francis** *Nicholson laid them out in 1696. Nicholson moved the Maryland capital to Annapolis. On the two highest points of land, he situated the State House and the official church, with circular streets surrounding them. Nicholson's plan may have influenced Pierre L'Enfant when he laid out Washington, D.C., a century later.*

members found it inconvenient being located on the extreme southern border of the province. Also, growth of St. Mary's had slowed, and it offered few amenities for visitors to Assembly sessions or court days. Its port had been eclipsed by Proctor's, which had been renamed Anne Arundel Town.

Still, St. Mary's might have survived as capital of Maryland had it not been for a revolution that saw Protestantism become England's official religion. Protestants in Maryland deposed Lord Baltimore's governor and seized control of the province. In 1692, the first royal governor of Maryland was appointed.

The second royal governor, Francis Nicholson, appointed in 1694, would change indelibly the face of Anne Arundel Town. On his arrival in the province, Nicholson recognized the limitations of St. Mary's as a provincial capital in terms of location and amenities. Even more significant from his perspective was the fact that the town was predominantly Catholic, an unsuitable circumstance. With the support of Nicholson, the mostly Protestant Assembly moved the capital to Anne Arundel Town in 1694.

The following year, Nicholson renamed the settlement Annapolis after the heir to the British throne, Princess Anne. With the assistance of surveyor Richard Beard, Nicholson also laid out streets for the new city. Around the two highest points of land he drew circles—one set aside for the Capitol, the other for the church.

Originally Church of England, St. Anne's was the official church of the Maryland colony. With the Revolution, most Annapolitans refused to attend a church headed by the King of England. They returned only after St. Anne's became part of the new Protestant Episcopal Church. During the Civil War, parishioners deserted St. Anne's because church leaders sided with the Union, contrary to local sentiment. Today, St. Anne's flourishes in relative tranquillity.

The church would be the Church of England, now the official religion of the province. Taxes were assessed to support the church, and laws were passed requiring attendance at services. However, attendance laws were not enforced rigorously. The seed of religious toleration would not wither easily.

Nicholson also was instrumental in founding King William's School (now St. John's College), and even put up some of his own money to help get it started.

In 1708, Annapolis received its royal charter as a city. With the election of the first mayor, Amos Garrett, and other officials, Annapolis became the seat of three levels of government: provincial, county, and city. Government became the business of the town; politics became its vocation and avocation.

Despite the efforts to establish a civilized society and Nicholson's grandiose plans, Annapolis remained a raw, rough, and sometimes bawdy frontier town through the first quarter of the 18th century. The city's streets were unpaved and ran with sewage. A large number of taverns existed to accommodate the transients drawn to Annapolis for Assembly sessions and court days.

Nicholson remained in Annapolis only briefly, departing in 1698 to become Royal Governor of Virginia. It is usual to express his Annapolis accomplishments in terms of streets and buildings. His most enduring legacy, however, may be political. In this most political of small towns, Nicholson established a tradition of bold initiative and enlightened action.

St. John's: Ancient School, "New Program"

McDowell Hall on the St. John's College campus was begun in 1742 as a "palace" for provincial Governor Thomas Bladen. Maryland's Assembly refused to appropriate money to complete construction of the grandiose mansion. For 40 years it sat half finished and was called "Bladen's Folly." Finally, it was turned over to St. John's, completed, and named after the college's first president, John McDowell.

Founded in 1696 as King William's School, St. John's is the third oldest college in the United States. During its years as King William's School, it led a hand-to-mouth existence. Neither the Lords Baltimore nor the Assembly saw fit to provide more than subsistence funding. Yet it survived and taught several generations of planters' sons "good letters and manners,...Latin, Greek, writing and the like."

With the Declaration of Independence, the school's name was changed to avoid any association with the English monarchy.

The 19th and 20th centuries saw numerous changes in curriculum as St. John's struggled to find a successful niche. The last and most significant change came in 1937.

Two young scholars, Stringfellow Barr and Scott Buchanan, concerned about the demise of classical, liberal education, came to St. John's as president and dean respectively. They instituted a "new program," radical by 20th century practice. Designed to educate students to think rather than to perform a certain type of work, the program is based on the reading of the great books of western civilization. All 400 St. John's students follow the same course of reading and discussing works of philosophy, history, literature, mathematics, and science.

Classes still meet in McDowell Hall. Commencement ceremonies are held under an ancient tulip poplar, "The Liberty Tree," where, according to legend, members of the Sons of Liberty met to plot rebellion against England.

▲ **The finest furniture and silver were imported from Europe for the great homes of Annapolis during "The Golden Age."** Men and women quickly adopted the latest European fashion in clothing and hair styles. The most adventuresome adopted gaudy Italian fashions and were referred to as "macaronis." A Frenchman visiting Annapolis wrote home that "female elegance here exceeds what is known in the provinces of France."

"Despite...the good life being enjoyed by many, an undercurrent of discontent could be heard in Annapolis."

"The Golden Age"

In 1749, a woman named Mrs. Baldwin died in Annapolis. What made her death noteworthy was that she was either 99 or 100 years old and had been born in Anne Arundel County. One reasonably could speculate that at the time of her death she had living children, grandchildren, great-grandchildren and, possibly, great-great-grandchildren. Cumulatively, that amounted to four or five generations of family members born in Maryland who most likely never set foot in England.

At the midpoint of the 18th century, the language, official religion, laws, and government of Annapolis were English, but its traditions increasingly were American. In Annapolis, as elsewhere in the colonies, American tradition and English government inexorably were moving toward conflict.

By this time, the rough town that Francis Nicholson laid out half a century earlier was changing dramatically. No native Americans

A handsome latch ▶ adorns the front door of the Chase-Lloyd House, one of the few great Annapolis homes which actually had the benefit of a professional architect. William Buckland completed the Chase-Lloyd House for the second owner, Edward Lloyd IV. Francis Scott Key, then a student at St. John's College, often called at the house to court and eventually marry Mary Tayloe Lloyd.

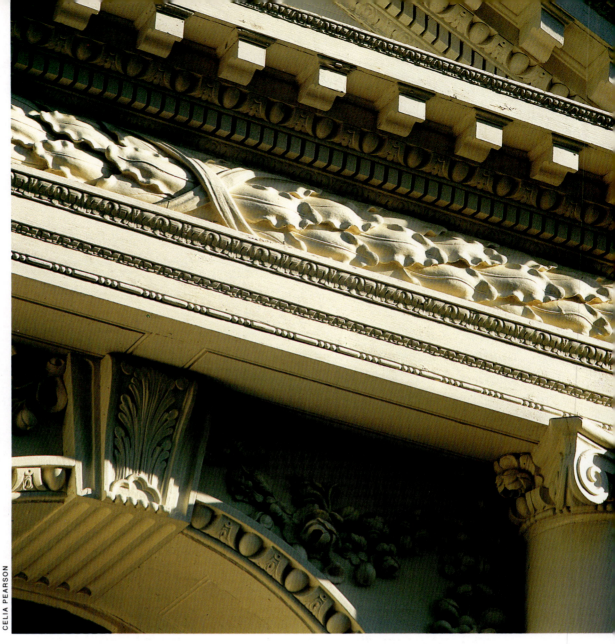

The doorway to the Hammond-Harwood House with its carved roses and elaborate moldings is a masterpiece of American art. The house, designed by William Buckland, is considered the finest example of Georgian architecture in the United States. Most Annapolis mansions were built without an architect's involvement, based on plans and drawings published in European books.

remained in the area, having fled to the north and west before the onslaught of European settlers.

The early homes of Annapolis were built primarily of wood and were modest and utilitarian in scale and style. By mid-century, more substantial structures were erected for middle-class Annapolitans. Rich merchants and planters started to build mansions.

The finest silver, furniture, and cloth from England were imported to decorate the grand homes. Paintings were required for the walls, and a young Annapolis saddlemaker and sign painter, Charles Willson Peale, started painting portraits of prominent citizens.

In contrast to the staid Puritans in New England and the reserved Quakers in Philadelphia, the gentry of Annapolis believed in dancing, gambling and, generally, enjoying the good life their wealth made possible. They attended theatrical performances and held countless balls. Wealthy planters from throughout the region came to Annapolis for the fall horse races and accompanying festivities. One of the regulars was George Washington.

The wealthy Annapolitans traveled in elegant carriages behind the finest horses. One planter made short water trips in a barge rowed by liveried servants. A visitor called the city "the Athens of America" and the era leading up to the Revolution was called "The Golden Age" of Annapolis.

Yet the era had its grim side. Largely dependent on a tobacco economy, slaves to work the fields were being imported from Africa and the West Indies and sold on the Annapolis city dock. By 1790, blacks constituted one third of Annapolis's population of 2,200. Most were slaves although the city had some free blacks.

Negroes weren't the only people sold on the city dock. A 1752 ad in *The Maryland Gazette*

The Banneker-Douglass Museum celebrates the history of blacks in Maryland. It is named after Benjamin Banneker, the free black surveyor who helped plan Washington, D.C., and Frederick Douglass, the escaped slave who became a prominent abolitionist, journalist, author, and public official.

announced the arrival of the ship *Friendship* with 300 Germans "who are offered for sale at Annapolis on the 14th of October." These indentured servants would be required to work for their purchasers for a certain number of years to pay off their passage to America.

Despite a booming economy and the good life being enjoyed by many, an undercurrent of discontent could be heard in Annapolis by the 1760s.

Catholics, Quakers, and others who did not embrace the Church of England attacked Maryland laws which denied them the full rights of citizenship and made them subject to discriminatory taxes. Devout Anglicans denounced arbitrary British laws and taxes.

Fueling this discontent were new ideas concerning the rights of man, equality, and republican government being voiced by philosophers in Western Europe and by Thomas Paine and Benjamin Franklin in America.

By the time Middleton Tavern opened for business in 1750, Annapolis was becoming one of the most urbane cities in America. Clubs flourished in Colonial Annapolis, and the most famous, The Tuesday Club, often met at Middleton's. A prominent member was Jonas Green, publisher of "The Maryland Gazette," one of the first newspapers in America. It continues to be published today.

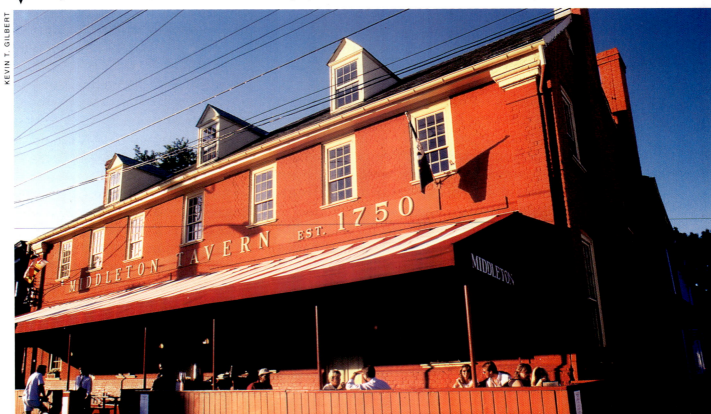

◀ **In its early days** the Shiplap House was a tavern. It was erected about 1713 when Annapolis was still a rough and bawdy frontier town. A clergyman wrote that the town was "a Sodom of uncleanliness & a pesthouse of iniquity." Owned by Historic Annapolis, the Shiplap House is open to the public.

In 1774, tea, and the hated British tax on it, were the catalysts for the most dramatic event in Annapolis leading up to the Revolution. The brig *Peggy Stewart* arrived in the Annapolis harbor with 2,000 pounds of tea. In anticipation of unloading the tea and the other cargo, the ship's owner, Annapolis merchant Anthony Stewart, paid the duty on the tea.

On learning of the tea aboard the ship and that the duty had been paid, Annapolis residents and many other Marylanders in town for court sessions were enraged. In the face of mounting hostility, including threats of being tarred and feathered, Stewart set the sails of his ship, ran it aground in the Severn River, and set fire to it, destroying ship and cargo.

Stewart's young daughter, Peggy, for whom the ship was named, may have watched it burn from the family's home on Hanover Street, known to this day as the Peggy Stewart House.

When it came time ultimately to declare liberty, four men prominent in Annapolis—Charles Carroll, William Paca, Samuel Chase, and Thomas Stone—represented Maryland at the Continental Congress in Philadelphia in 1776, and signed the Declaration of Independence. Annapolis saw no fighting in the war that followed, but many members of its militia died on distant battlefields.

With the end of the war, Congress met in Annapolis from November 26, 1783, to August 13, 1784, making the city briefly the capital of the United States. George Washington came to the State House to return his commission as commander-in-chief of the Continental Army to civil authorities, thus assuring the supremacy of civil government in the new nation.

The Treaty of Paris, officially ending the Revolutionary War and obtaining formal British recognition of American independence, was ratified by Congress in Annapolis.

The Annapolis Convention of 1786 was called to consider trade problems among the states. The convention was poorly attended, but two of its participants, Alexander Hamilton and James Madison, drafted a document urging all 13 states to send delegates to a convention to consider means to make "the federal government adequate to the exigencies of the Union." The convention in Philadelphia in 1787 produced the United States Constitution.

Although it had its genesis in Annapolis, William Paca refused to support the Constitution. As a signer of the Declaration of Independence,

his refusal threatened ratification. Paca felt the Constitution failed to protect individual rights. He agreed to give his support only after receiving assurances that the Constitution would be amended to meet his objections. Those amendments, ultimately adopted, were the Bill of Rights. Among those rights was religious toleration. The seed planted more than 150 years earlier in Maryland at last had borne fruit.

As the 18th century drew to a close, the small but very political city that Francis Nicholson created a century earlier could look back with pride on having contributed to three of the most important documents of all time: the Declaration of Independence, the United States Constitution, and the Bill of Rights.

◀ **Tents for a party flank the rear entrance of** the mansion built by William Paca. It is one of four existing houses in Annapolis once owned by signers of the Declaration of Independence. Paca and other wealthy Annapolitans entertained lavishly. A student of the era said that "they drank punch out of vast, costly bowls from Japan, or sipped Madiera half a century old." An Englishman wrote home, "I hardly know of a town in England as desirable...as Annapolis."

Dr. Upton Scott, a Northern Irish physician, ▶ came to Annapolis in 1753 with Governor Horatio Sharpe. He received a number of lucrative public offices and built this house in the 1760s. Like some other wealthy Annapolitans, Scott remained loyal to England during the Revolution, but remained in Annapolis. Ironically, Mrs. Scott's nephew, Francis Scott Key, author of "The Star-Spangled Banner," lived here while a student at St. John's College. The house on Shipwright Street continues to be occupied as a private home.

▲ **To** *celebrate Maryland's ratification of the U.S. Constitution, Baltimore craftsmen built a 15-foot, fully-rigged boat, "The Federalist." This replica is displayed in the State House.*

Maryland's State ▷ *House has two Senate chambers. This one serves contemporary legislators. The old Senate chamber, now a museum, is the more famous. That's where Washington resigned his commission and the Treaty of Paris, ending the Revolution, was signed.*

▲ **W**ashington's resignation as commander-in-chief, one of the most emotional and significant events of American history, is memorialized in a painting in the building where it took place.

◀ **T**he third Maryland State House on this site was started in 1771 and expanded in 1858, 1886, and 1902. It has the largest wooden dome in the United States.

◀ **T**he Maryland House of Delegates, which meets in this chamber, traditionally has been the more raucous and uncontrollable of the two houses. In Colonial times, the elected delegates once refused to comply with a "command" from the King of England.

19

▲ **The Chase-Lloyd House was started in 1769 by Samuel Chase, a fiery revolutionary and one of** the four Maryland signers of the Declaration of Independence. Two years after construction began, Chase realized he could not afford to complete the house, and sold it to Edward Lloyd IV. The house is famed for its elaborate carved moldings and cornices, and cantilevered main stairway framing a huge Palladian window. The house was occupied by descendants of the Lloyd family and others until 1886 when the last private owner, Hester Ann Chase Ridout, bequeathed it to be used as a home for elderly women, which it is today. It is open to the public on a limited basis.

"Of far greater significance than what happened in Annapolis during the 150 years beginning in 1800 is what didn't happen."

A Sleepy Southern Town

By the beginning of the 19th century, Annapolis had been eclipsed by Baltimore as the major port and dominant city of Maryland. Passed over as the potential capital of the United States, Annapolis had to fight an attempt by Baltimore to usurp its status as the capital of Maryland.

The United States Naval Academy was established in 1845 on the banks of the Severn and the Civil War wreaked havoc in Annapolis, but for 150 years from 1800 to 1950 little else of significance happened in the once vital city. Annapolis took on the aura of a sleepy southern town.

Like many slave-holding, border-state cities, the sympathies of Annapolis were more southern than northern when Abraham Lincoln ran for President in 1860. Lincoln received only one vote in Annapolis, three in Anne Arundel County.

A tour guide relaxes in his 18th-century garb. Well-made clothing, often imported from England, was a valuable commodity in Colonial times. Frequently, clothes were specifically bequeathed in wills along with such items as jewelry and real estate.

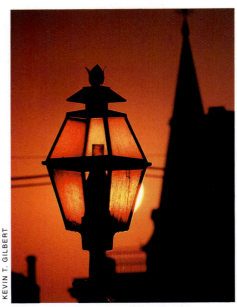

▲ **M**ajor 18th-century events were celebrated by placing candles in every window. Modern street lights, in Colonial style, suffice today.

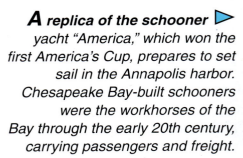

A replica of the schooner ▷ yacht "America," which won the first America's Cup, prepares to set sail in the Annapolis harbor. Chesapeake Bay-built schooners were the workhorses of the Bay through the early 20th century, carrying passengers and freight.

Secession of the southern states after Lincoln's election created a near panic in Annapolis. Union troops under the command of General Benjamin Butler arrived to set up camp on the Naval Academy grounds and to seize other strategic locations. For the duration of the war Annapolis was an occupied city. It became the site of a huge military hospital and a center for reception of Union soldiers captured by the Confederates and then exchanged (paroled was the term generally used in that era) for Confederate prisoners held by the Union.

The hospital, housed mainly in tents and frame buildings hurriedly erected, ultimately overflowed the grounds of the Academy. The St. John's College campus was taken over by the army to be both a hospital and a reception center for paroled prisoners. With as many as 6,000 parolees arriving on some days, the college grounds also proved inadequate. A new camp was set up on the western outskirts of Annapolis, in an area still called Parole.

Like every city in America, Annapolis felt the pain of war in the loss of men killed in action— some fighting for the North, some for the South.

In 1864, the Maryland General Assembly, which had moved out of occupied Annapolis to Frederick in western Maryland, adopted a new state constitution. It freed all slaves in the state, including 500 in Annapolis. After the war, a viable

◀ **Tombstones in the Annapolis** National Cemetery mostly mark graves of Union soldiers who died in Annapolis hospitals during the Civil War. Equally as tragic were the circumstances of many local residents torn by conflicting loyalties. One was elderly Commodore Isaac Mayo, a hero of the Mexican War. When southern states seceded, Mayo wrote a letter of resignation to President Lincoln saying, "It was the hope of my old age that I might die as I have lived, an officer in the Navy of a free government." Although many officers were allowed to resign, Lincoln ordered Mayo dishonorably discharged. Mayo never learned of Lincoln's decision. He died the same day. Dishonored by his government, Mayo remains a hero in Maryland.

black community developed with its own businesses, schools, and churches. In 1873, Annapolis elected William H. Butler as an alderman, the first black to hold elected office in Maryland.

Through World War II, growth was slow in Annapolis. Government and politics remained the principal industry. The Naval Academy provided jobs for many. The marine industry survived, serving Chesapeake Bay watermen instead of the oceangoing traffic of the Colonial era.

Of far greater significance than *what happened* in Annapolis during the 150 years beginning in 1800 is *what didn't happen*: no devastating fires wiping out whole blocks of buildings, no industrial development requiring large factories, no businesses significant enough to warrant high-rise buildings.

A century and one-half in the backwater of American expansionism had left Annapolis an older, somewhat rundown version of the glorious city Francis Nicholson envisioned. In 1949, as the 300th anniversary of the original settlement at Providence was celebrated in Annapolis, the 18th-century city described as "the Athens of America" remained surprisingly intact. By and large, the old mansions and homes, taverns, warehouses, churches, and government buildings were standing, still being used for the purposes for which they had been erected years earlier.

▲ **Reynolds Tavern, built on Church Circle** in the mid-18th century, was painstakingly restored by a visionary Annapolitan, Paul Pearson. Once again, it's open for business.

Overleaf: *The* ▶
Academy "yard." Photo
by Kevin T. Gilbert.

"Every vista...is evocative of the ideals of service to country, dedication to duty, and self-sacrifice."

The United States Naval Academy

Few experiences compare with watching a parade at the United States Naval Academy. From the grandstand on Worden Field, the Academy yard stretches in verdant splendor, stately buildings against a manicured landscape. Beyond, Navy yawls with billowing spinnakers ply the Severn. Flags flap in the breeze. Sunlight dances from 4,000 bayonets. The band plays *Anchors Aweigh*. The brigade of midshipmen, all in glistening white, navy blue, and gold, passes in review.

It's tempting to conclude that such a scene is the essence of the Naval Academy. It is part of it. But to experience fully what this place on the Severn River is all about, you have to leave the sunlight and descend into the half-light of the crypt beneath the Naval Academy Chapel chancel. There, in the presence of the earthly remains of John Paul Jones, you can begin to grasp the full

◀ **Noon formation** in the courtyard of Bancroft Hall brings together the Brigade of Midshipmen. All 4,000 midshipmen live in Bancroft, the world's largest dormitory.

Led by ▶ their midshipmen officers, a company marches to Worden Field for a dress parade.

PHOTOS BY KEVIN T. GILBERT

significance of the United States Naval Academy.

The Naval Academy is a crucible for warriors. That is what it was planned to be. But it has become much more than that. It is hallowed ground to all who cherish American freedom and would pay tribute to those whose exploits and sacrifices have preserved it.

John Paul Jones was an advocate of a professional school for naval officers almost from the time that he sailed against the British during the Revolution and issued his famous response to a demand to surrender: "I have not yet begun to fight."

The training of officers was a haphazard process in the early days of the United States Navy. Boys, some as young as 12, were placed aboard ships as midshipmen, originally a term used to describe a seaman assigned to remain amidships to relay orders forward and aft. What training the boys received varied greatly from ship to ship. Yet Congress refused to provide funds for a naval school despite the support of seven successive secretaries of the Navy.

A brilliant and resourceful secretary, George Bancroft, ultimately found a way around Congress. Appointed in the spring of 1845, Bancroft was convinced of the need for a naval school. He learned the Army was willing to relinquish Fort Severn, guarding the entrance to the Annapolis harbor, and quickly acquired it. Rather than seek a special appropriation from Congress for the school, Bancroft simply suspended certain other naval operations and applied the money saved to fund the new school. By fall of 1845, 56 midshipmen arrived to begin classes at Fort Severn.

Midshipmen received one year of classroom instruction, were sent to the fleet for up to two and one-half years, and then returned for a final year of classes.

By the 1860s, the Naval School had been officially renamed the Naval Academy. Midshipmen were required to wear uniforms and participate in close-order drill. The two-year curriculum interrupted by sea duty had been replaced by four consecutive years of study for the 300 midshipmen then in attendance.

Nothing in the history of the Naval Academy or the Navy was more traumatic than the Civil War. It pitted midshipman against midshipman and officer against officer. It uprooted the Academy from Annapolis with a possibility that it might never return.

As one after another of the southern states

Since the arrival of its first superintendent, Franklin Buchanan, in 1845, the fundamental mission of the Academy has remained the training of fighting men (and more recently, women). Buchanan, a Marylander, resigned from the U.S. Navy when southern states seceded. He rose to admiral in the Confederate Navy, and at ▼ one time commanded the famed ironclad, "Merrimac."

◄ **Author William O. Stevens** called the Academy "a Valhalla of American heroes and a record of naval history." Among the graves, the monuments, and the artifacts throughout the Academy, nothing is more inspirational than Commodore Oliver Hazard Perry's flag from the War of 1812. Beneath it are the names of all deceased Academy graduates.

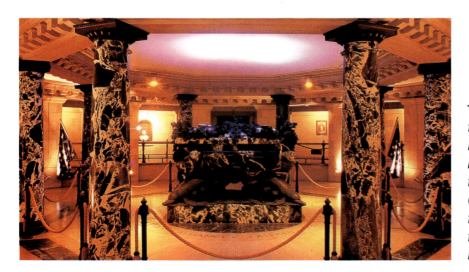

◄ **John Paul Jones,** the "father of the Navy," is entombed in heroic grandeur in the crypt of the Academy Chapel. In life, Jones fought unsuccessfully for a professional naval school.

▲ *Flying F-16s, the Navy's Blue Angels perform their aerial acrobatics annually in Annapolis during Commissioning Week. The event draws tens of thousands of spectators.*

seceded in 1861, midshipmen and officers from those states began submitting their resignations from the U.S. Navy. Choosing sides never was easy. Two brothers from Virginia debated their options before one elected to remain with the Union and the other joined the Confederates.

Anti-Union rioting had broken out in Baltimore when, on April 19, 1861, a Massachusetts regiment under the command of General Benjamin Butler arrived unexpectedly by ship at the Academy. Butler's primary objective was to protect Washington, secondarily to occupy Annapolis. By April 24, the Academy was an armed camp with three regiments of Union troops bivouacked on its grounds. To the Academy superintendent and the Navy Secretary, it seemed neither prudent nor practical to continue classes in Annapolis.

On April 27, those midshipmen who were pro-Union boarded ship and sailed to Newport, Rhode Island. There, in cramped quarters, the Naval Academy remained for the duration of the war. With the end of hostilities in 1865, Newport and a number of other cities bid to be the permanent location of the Academy. The Secretary of the Navy, however, was determined to restore the Academy to Annapolis. By October, 1865, the Navy had reclaimed the sadly-abused Academy grounds and resumed classes.

Twenty-six former midshipmen—20 Union and 6 Confederate—were killed or died of injuries in the war. Among the many graduates cited for heroism was 23-year-old George Dewey.

If the Civil War was a low point in the history of the Academy, the Spanish-American War in 1898 may rank as one of the highest. Not only was the United States victorious, but the Navy with Academy graduates serving in the highest ranks was conspicuously successful. With his defeat of the Spanish at Manila Bay, Dewey became the greatest United States naval hero since John Paul Jones.

In 1905, the remains of Jones were discovered in a Paris cemetery just as the Naval Academy was experiencing a boom in new construction in the aftermath of the Spanish-American War. The Academy's new chapel then under construction seemed the most fitting place

◀ **A Blue Angel banks into** a turn before a run down the Severn River. In a matter of seconds, the F-16 will run the length of the seawall and disappear in a deafening roar. Historically, the Academy has been on the cutting edge of science and technology. In 1911, three planes arrived in crates at the Academy. One was unpacked and assembled that afternoon. The next day, Lieutenant John Rodgers took off in the open cockpit, did a few turns, buzzed the field, and founded Navy aviation. Graduate Albert A. Michelson made the most precise measurement ever obtained of the speed of light at the Academy. In 1907 he became the first American awarded the Nobel Prize.

to inter America's first naval hero. Jones was laid to rest in the crypt in 1913.

Other heroes are buried in the Academy cemetery. Monuments to their exploits and the exploits of others are everywhere to be seen throughout the Academy yard and within its buildings. None is more inspirational than Commodore Oliver Hazard Perry's flag flown in the Battle of Lake Erie in 1813 with its message fundamental to all Navy warriors: "DON'T GIVE UP THE SHIP."

Formal monuments aside, every building, every vista at the Naval Academy is evocative of the ideals of service to country, dedication to duty, and self-sacrifice. This is where Dewey (class of 1858) and Albert A. Michelson (1874), first American to win the Nobel Prize, practiced close-order drill. Here you can walk in the footsteps of World War II leaders William F. "Bull" Halsey (1904) and Chester Nimitz ('05). This is the school that produced Hyman Rickover ('22), "father" of the nuclear navy; astronaut Alan B. Shepard, Jr. ('45), first American in space who later walked on the moon; and President Jimmy Carter ('46). United States Senator John McCain ('58) credited his Academy training with helping him survive five years as a prisoner of war in Vietnam.

In the footsteps of a company of midshipmen marching across this yard, you may hear echoes of the footsteps of more than 900 former midshipmen killed in the line of duty during the past 150 years. In the young faces passing by, you may see images of the 73 Academy graduates awarded the Congressional Medal of Honor. That's what the United States Naval Academy is all about.

▲ **Young men and women arrive at the Academy** to begin their lives as midshipmen. Carrying just-issued uniforms in bags and wearing their distinctive "Dixie Cup" hats, these fourth classmen, or plebes as they are called, head for dormitory assignments. Later in the day, in front of friends and family, they will swear "to defend the Constitution of the United States against all enemies, foreign and domestic."

PHOTOS BY KEVIN T. GILBERT

▲ **Just the first of many indignities to** be endured during "plebe summer" is the military haircut. It takes only about a minute.

◀ **All 4,000 midshipmen eat at** one sitting in mammoth King Hall. Along with a staggering amount of naval and Academy lore, plebes are required to memorize the day's menus for each meal to be repeated at the request of any upper classman.

*Come explore America's Parks with us!
With over 100 titles to choose from,
see why we are your #1 choice!*

Rush me a *free* color catalog.	**1-800-626-9673**
Can't wait . . . I'm calling you for more information.	**1-702-433-3415**
Tell me about your Translation Packages.	fax: **1-702-433-3420**
Tell me about your educational teacher resources.	

_____ First Name _____ (Please Print) _____ Last Name

Address _____

City _____ State _____

Zip _____ Country _____

Day Phone _____

Fax _____

❑ Personal Use ❑ Retail ❑ Teacher

Other _____

Comments _____

BUSINESS REPLY MAIL
FIRST-CLASS MAIL PERMIT NO. 3005 LAS VEGAS NV

POSTAGE WILL BE PAID BY THE ADDRESSEE

KC PUBLICATIONS
3245 E PATRICK LANE SUITE A
P O BOX 94558
LAS VEGAS NV 89195-0196

NO POSTAGE
NECESSARY
IF MAILED
IN THE
UNITED STATES

▲ **T**oday's midshipmen never will go to war aboard sailing ships, but learning to sail remains a part of their training. When the formal training is over, many midshipmen continue to sail in competition or for recreation. They compete in intercollegiate events, local races in Annapolis, and national and international competition. Through the first half of the 20th century, large sailing ships were berthed at the Academy. They were used as training vessels and supplemental living quarters. At one time, "Old Ironsides," the venerable "USS Constitution," was part of the Academy fleet.

◀ **C**limbing the greased Herndon Monument during Commissioning Week in May is the final rite of passage for plebes. When a plebe places a "Dixie Cup" hat atop the monument, fourth class members officially become third classmen. Within a few weeks they'll begin their first summer cruise aboard a warship.

▗ **The Brigade of Midshipmen takes** the field in Navy-Marine Corps Memorial Stadium. The pre-game "march-on," directed by a midshipman in the stands, is a key element of the pageantry surrounding Navy football. Parachute jumps by Navy Seals, or a jet flyover may add to the excitement.

The Naval Academy Band marches in a Memorial Day ▶ parade in downtown Annapolis. The band, made up of active-duty Navy personnel rather than midshipmen, performs at Academy functions and national functions in Washington and holds a popular summer series of concerts on the city dock.

No public money ▶ goes to support Navy football or other varsity sports. Funds come from the Naval Academy Athletic Association, a private organization. The Army-Navy football game is its largest source of revenue. Whatever the overall record, a Navy victory over Army is tantamount to a winning season.

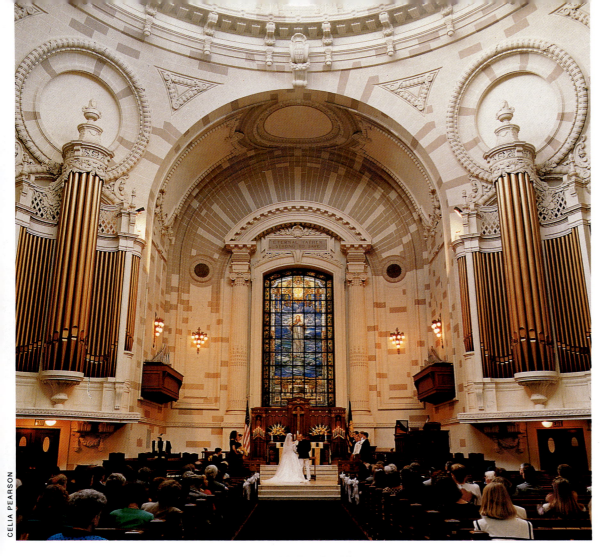

◀ **In the beaux arts** splendor of the Naval Academy Chapel, a newly-commissioned Marine second lieutenant exchanges vows with his bride. Prohibited from marrying while midshipmen, many graduates march directly from their commissioning ceremony to the altar. Weddings are scheduled, and conducted, with military precision.

▲ **Commissioning and wedding over, ensign** and wife, family and friends will celebrate at an Annapolis hotel or home.

Bill Clinton, like other presidents, has come ▶ to the Academy for commissioning ceremonies. Graduates, however, may be less impressed by presidents than by the fact they have completed four tough years.

▲ *From the front yard of the Chase-Lloyd House, the imposing facade of Hammond-Harwood with its famous doorway presides over Maryland Avenue. The house was acquired in 1938 by the Hammond-Harwood Association, thwarting an effort by Henry Ford to purchase it and have it moved brick-by-brick to Michigan. John D. Rockefeller also was interested in Annapolis in that era. When local residents objected to some of his proposed zoning changes, he turned his attention to Williamsburg for his grand restoration project.*

"As always a living, vital, working city, not a 20th-century re-creation."

"The Second Golden Age"

Miss Lucy and Miss Hester Harwood were aging, suspicious spinsters. As legend has it, they drove off small boys intruding on their garden with an antique dueling pistol. They filed countless unsuccessful suits against adult neighbors they perceived as intent on denying them what was rightfully theirs. They survived in part on food left on their doorsteps by neighbors.

In post-World War I Annapolis, the sisters Harwood were true eccentrics. While they may have had no income, they lived in the most exquisite house built in the town's "Golden Age" surrounded by priceless antique furnishings and portraits by Charles Willson Peale.

What the sisters lacked in ready cash, they made up for with a surfeit of pride. No matter how hard the times, the sisters maintained the charade that they were well off. Neighbors who

◄ **Hundreds of buildings** from the 17th and 18th centuries, some of them tiny homes, line downtown Annapolis streets. Approval of a Historic District Ordinance by Annapolis voters in 1969 was one of the most significant achievements of Historic Annapolis. It set up a commission with authority to approve or reject all proposed demolition, alteration, or construction in a one-square-mile area. This saved the city from indiscriminate redevelopment.

▲ "*E*go Alley" cuts into the heart of downtown Annapolis from Spa Creek. It gets its name from the challenge it presents to skippers of large boats who want to impress passengers or strollers on the dock with their ability to enter the waterway, cruise to its end, turn the boat around and exit without leaving any hull paint on the bulkheads. Many try, but not all succeed. At the head of the alley is the restored Colonial Market House. Brick-paved Main Street is to the left. In the 1950s, before restoration, a gas station stood in the circle now occupied by the flagpole. Many a boater arriving in town will head immediately to Fawcett's, referred to often as the "Tiffany's" of marine supply stores.

◀ **The home of Charles Carroll of Carrolton** stands majestically on the banks of Spa Creek. The richest man in America, Carroll was denied public office because of his Catholic faith. He fought discriminatory laws, and ultimately became a leader in the Revolutionary cause. Before his death in 1832, Carroll was the last surviving signer of the Declaration of Independence.

left them food did not expect their charity to be acknowledged. Disposing of any of the valuable furnishings, paintings, or their home, the Hammond-Harwood House, was out of the question.

Miss Lucy died and Miss Hester passed away a few years later in 1924. The Hammond-Harwood House was sold at auction. Its purchase by St. John's College in a way marked the beginning of the successful preservationist movement in Annapolis. The college ultimately found it impractical to maintain the house. However, in 1938, it was acquired and opened to the public by the new Hammond-Harwood Association.

The fierce pride of the eccentric Harwood sisters had succeeded in preserving their 18th-century home during an era when other mansions of "The Golden Age" were being abused. Around the corner, the noble Paca House was merely a facade for a 200-room hotel, Carvel Hall, rudely attached to its rear.

Some individual historic properties in Annapolis were being preserved and maintained by private owners or institutions, but no viable, citywide preservation organization emerged until 1952 with the founding of Historic Annapolis, Inc. (now the Historic Annapolis Foundation). At the time, Annapolis appeared ready to emerge from its 150-year slumber. Developers eyed the waterfront, eager to replace 18th-century buildings with modern structures, including a high-rise hotel.

The challenge for the new organization was to convince local residents and business owners that preservation of the 18th-century city was both culturally essential and economically advantageous. Fortunately, Historic Annapolis had as its moving force St. Clair Wright, a woman with the vision of Francis Nicholson, the courage of the signers of the Declaration of Independence, and the resourcefulness of George Bancroft.

The results of Historic Annapolis's efforts are everywhere to be observed. The gas station, which in the 1950s occupied the traffic circle on the city dock, is gone. So too are the utility lines that marred vistas on State Circle and Main Street. The Market House, for years boarded up, is restored and reopened.

Nearly 500 homes and other buildings were saved directly or indirectly by Historic Annapolis.

The crowning achievement of Mrs. Wright was the restoration of the Paca House and garden. When Carvel Hall Hotel was put up for sale in 1965, Historic Annapolis purchased it. The frame portions of the hotel were torn down and the Paca House was restored. Archeology helped to reveal the original contour of the garden beneath the hotel and its parking lot. A portrait of Paca with the garden as background provided other evidence of the garden as it existed in Paca's day. The site was excavated to its original depth and Paca's garden was recreated.

The U.S. Sailboat ▶ Show at the city dock was started in 1970 as an experiment by a couple of local businessmen. Annapolis needed a boat show, they believed, but the city had no building large enough for a traditional show. They hit on the then-novel idea of putting the boats in the water. So large was the response, every restaurant in downtown Annapolis ran out of food the first night of the show. The U.S. Power Boat Show made its debut in 1972.

By the 1960s, Annapolis was being rediscovered, and not only by tourists interested in visiting Colonial homes and the Naval Academy. The Annapolis harbor and its easy access to Chesapeake Bay beckoned boaters from throughout the mid-Atlantic.

Those who loved sailing found Annapolis especially appealing. The bay with all its tributaries, safe harbors, and quaint towns offered unparalleled cruising. Sailing races were held weekly.

The only thing Annapolis lacked in terms of sailing attractions was an annual boat show. The town had no hall large enough to accommodate a traditional indoor boat show, so some local businessmen conjured up the idea of putting the boats in the water at the city dock. The world's first in-water Sailboat Show was held in 1970. Its success was instantaneous. Within two years, a companion show, the United States Power Boat Show, was started. The two shows, held in October, are billed as the "world's largest."

Whether they came for the boat shows, weekend sailing, a Navy football game, a stroll

▲ **Big-city-dwelling sailors began keeping boats like "Dancer" in Annapolis for easy** access to the Bay. Finding that the town offered better living as well as sailing, many subsequently moved here, renovating old homes and building new ones.

through the Paca garden, or a session of the General Assembly, out-of-town visitors filled the streets of downtown Annapolis by the 1970s. Long boarded-up storefronts reopened as restaurants and boutiques. As promised by St. Clair Wright, the economic advantage of preservation was realized.

The 1980s witnessed the arrival of what *National Geographic* called "The Second Golden Age" of Annapolis. Tiny 18th-century frame houses in the Historic District sold for hundreds of thousands of dollars to buyers who spent lavishly to restore them. Every vacant lot on the water became the site of a new million-dollar home.

At the end of its fourth century, Annapolis has come full circle.

Skippered sailboats and bare boats, sail and ▷
power, can be chartered or rented by the hour. Sailing instruction is available. The Annapolis Sailing School, with branches in Florida and the Caribbean, graduates 7,000 new sailors some years.

◀ **Schoolchildren on tour** will be taught to identify the various types of architecture that mark the 350-year history of Annapolis. Preservation of Victorian buildings, such as the one the children are passing, is as important to Historic Annapolis as preserving older structures. Good 20th-century architecture is as valued as Georgian. However, all new construction must be harmonious and in scale with historic buildings.

The Maryland ▶ Governor's Mansion was built after the Civil War as a Victorian building with a mansard roof. Later, it was renovated to its current Georgian appearance. Such renovation would be discouraged by Historic Annapolis today. Also discouraged in the Historic District is construction of new, ersatz colonial buildings.

◀ **In the Paca House with** a photograph of its garden in hand, St. Clair Wright was in her element. Mrs. Wright led Historic Annapolis during its most productive years. More important than the buildings she saved, was the fact that she taught a generation of Annapolitans that understanding and appreciating their past was the key to their future.

As it was in the days of the signers of the Declaration of Independence, it is today the most political of cities, still the seat of three levels of government. Such radical ideas as freedom of religion and democratic government, which gained early voice in Annapolis, now are secure in the land.

Annapolis continues to be, as it was in Colonial days, a mecca for visitors attracted by the great 18th-century homes and the opportunities for recreation and entertainment.

It remains the crucible for warriors created by Bancroft, and the Valhalla of naval heroes.

It is the glorious city envisioned by Francis Nicholson and saved, in large measure, by the work of St. Clair Wright; as always a living, vital, working city, not a 20th-century re-creation.

Local residents will tell you that what John Smith said back in 1608 remains true today: "Heaven and earth have never agreed better to frame a place for man's habitation."

SUGGESTED READING

ANDERSON, ELIZABETH B. Photographs by M.E. Warren. *A Walk Through History*. Centreville, Maryland: Tidewater Publishers, 1984.

MIDDLETON, ARTHUR PIERCE. Photographs by N. Jane Iseley. *Annapolis on the Chesapeake*. Annapolis, Maryland: Historic Annapolis, Inc.; and Greensboro, North Carolina: Legacy Publications, 1988.

SWEETMAN, JACK. *The U.S. Naval Academy*. Annapolis, Maryland: Naval Institute Press, 1979.

▲ **Local residents dress up to celebrate the** 200th anniversary of the signing of the Treaty of Paris. The treaty, which formally ended the Revolutionary War, was signed while Congress met in Annapolis, making the city briefly the capital of the new nation. It represented the first time England formally recognized the United States.

▲ **Founding fathers of the United States** passed this way, some to do business at the old Maryland Treasury Building (to the right of the large tree), the oldest surviving public building in the state.

▲ **Navy people for years have called** Annapolis "Crabtown." While the sobriquet is used in a mildly derogatory way, catching and eating Chesapeake Bay crabs is a way of life to Annapolitans. Getting meat out of the crab requires skill and patience, but locals claim that nothing matches its taste.

Dogwoods bloom on the State House grounds. Across the street is the house of Robert Shaw, the most renowned cabinetmaker in Colonial Annapolis. One ▼ of his bookcase desks is in the White House.

PHOTOS BY KEVIN T. GILBERT

▲ **In the 1950s, boarded-up storefronts were common in downtown Annapolis. Now, those same** buildings house restaurants and upscale boutiques, an economic side effect of historic preservation. These buildings facing the harbor are considered fine examples of commercial Victorian architecture.

▲ **A local resident dresses up** for a Colonial fair at the Charles Carroll House.

A used book store, a smoke ▷ shop, boutiques, and a number of antique shops make Maryland Avenue one of the town's most attractive commercial districts.

▲ **Fireworks explode over Annapolis Harbor on July 4th celebrating American independence.**
During the Revolutionary War to secure that independence, no fighting occurred in the city or its vicinity, but the Marquis de Lafayette encamped with his troops in Annapolis, capturing the hearts of many ladies.

From its earliest days, Annapolis attracted visitors who came to conduct governmental business, practice politics, and have a good time. That remains as true today as it was in George Washington's time. Most astonishing is that the visitor sees a city remarkably similar to the one Washington saw. Annapolis is not a 20th-century re-creation of an 18th-century city. It is authentic, with hundreds of buildings from the Colonial and Revolutionary eras still standing. It is not a museum, but a living, vital city. Houses once occupied by Colonial governors or dedicated revolutionaries are home to modern families. In public buildings where the words of Jefferson and Madison resounded, contemporary issues are debated. Taverns that entertained the "fathers" of our country still serve food and drink to their "sons and daughters."

◀ **Flags fly proudly over the** State House, once the seat of an English governor, once capitol of the United States.

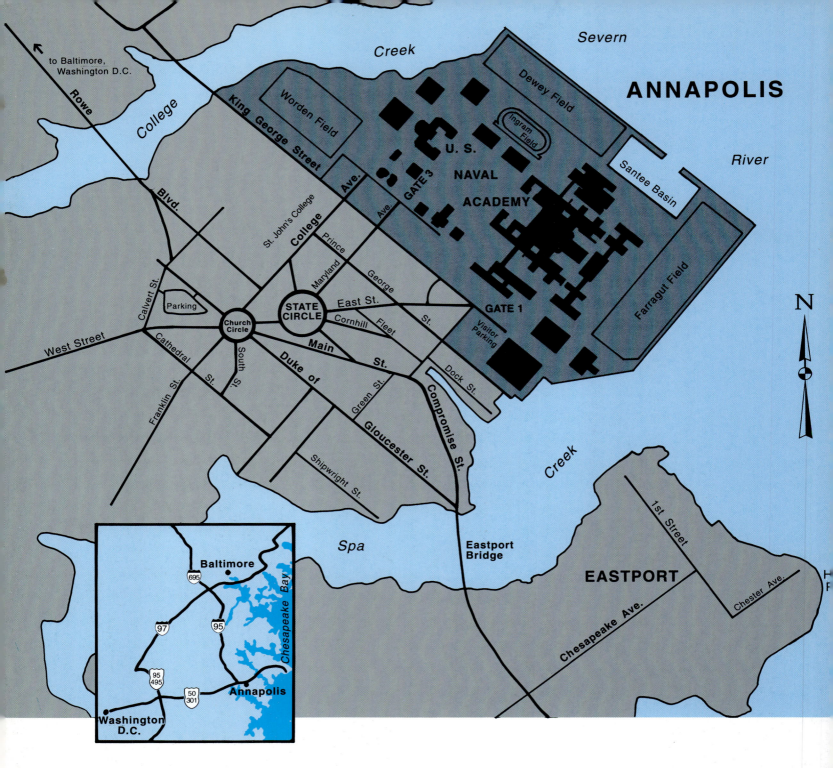

Books on national park areas in "The Story Behind the Scenery" series are: Acadia, Alcatraz Island, Arches, Big Bend, Biscayne, Blue Ridge Parkway, Bryce Canyon, Canyon de Chelly, Canyonlands, Cape Cod, Capitol Reef, Channel Islands, Civil War Parks, Colonial, Crater Lake, Death Valley, Denali, Devils Tower, Dinosaur, Everglades, Fort Clatsop, Gettysburg, Glacier, Glen Canyon-Lake Powell, Grand Canyon, Grand Canyon-North Rim, Grand Teton, Great Basin, Great Smoky Mountains, Haleakala, Hawaii Volcanoes, Independence, Lake Mead-Hoover Dam, Lassen Volcanic, Lincoln Parks, Mammoth Cave, Mesa Verde, Mount Rainier, Mount Rushmore, National Park Service, National Seashores, North Cascades, Olympic, Petrified Forest, Redwood, Rocky Mountain, Scotty's Castle, Sequoia & Kings Canyon, Shenandoah, Statue of Liberty, Theodore Roosevelt, Virgin Islands, Yellowstone, Yosemite, Zion.

Additional books in "The Story Behind the Scenery" series are: Annapolis, Big Sur, California Gold Country, California Trail, Colorado Plateau, Columbia River Gorge, Fire: A Force of Nature, Grand Circle Adventure, John Wesley Powell, Kauai, Lake Tahoe, Las Vegas, Lewis & Clark, Monument Valley, Mormon Temple Square, Mormon Trail, Mount St. Helens, Nevada's Red Rock Canyon, Nevada's Valley of Fire, Oregon Trail, Oregon Trail Center, Santa Catalina, Santa Fe Trail, Sharks, Sonoran Desert, U.S. Virgin Islands, Water: A Gift of Nature, Whales.

A companion series of national park areas is the NEW "in pictures...The Continuing Story." This series has **Translation Packages**, providing each title with a complete text both in English and, individually, a second language, German, French, or Japanese. Selected titles in both this series and our other books are available in up to five additional languages. Call (800-626-9673), fax (702-433-3420), or write to the address below.

Published by KC Publications, 3245 E. Patrick Ln., Suite A, Las Vegas, NV 89120.

Inside back cover: *The sun rises over the Chesapeake Bay Bridge. Photo by Kevin T. Gilbert.*

Back cover: *A Naval Academy yard patrol boat begins an instructional cruise. Photo by Kevin T. Gilbert.*

Created, Designed and Published in the U.S.A.
Printed by Dong-A Publishing and Printing, Seoul, Korea
Color Separations by Kedia/Kwangyangsa Co., Ltd.